Oliver
Doodle Dandy

Written by Todd M. Zimmermann

Illustrated by Kyle Hernandez

This book is dedicated to:

Theodore Zimmermann
U.S. Army
WWI

Theodore H. Zimmermann
U.S. Army
Korean War

Norbert Hoerst
U.S. Army Air Force
WWII

Helmuth "Schimmel" Eberhardt
U.S. Army
WWII

Leroy Zimmermann
U.S. Army
WWII

Doris Olmstead Zimmermann
U.S. Navy
WWII

Arno Albrecht
U.S. Army
Korean War

Mike McLean
U.S. Army
Vietnam War
Milwaukee Fire Department

Rick Zimmermann
U.S. Army

Karen Zimmermann
U.S. Army

David Zimmermann
Milwaukee Fire
Department

Jacob Kazar
U.S. Air Force

Kevin Menzer
U.S. Army
Iraq War

Carson Ostermann
U.S. Marines

This book is further dedicated to all those who have served and are serving in our armed services, as well as all first responders and healthcare professionals who protect and serve our great nation.

School had ended weeks ago and now the family was busy getting ready for their annual Fourth of July picnic. Mom and Dad were busy decorating, while Henry and Holly were busy on their devices.

4th of July ★

"Will you please go up to the attic and get our flags?" Mom asked Henry and Holly.

Henry and Holly were so involved with their devices, they didn't hear Mom's request, and so she asked again: "Will you please go to the attic and get our flags?"

This time Henry answered, "In a minute, Mom."

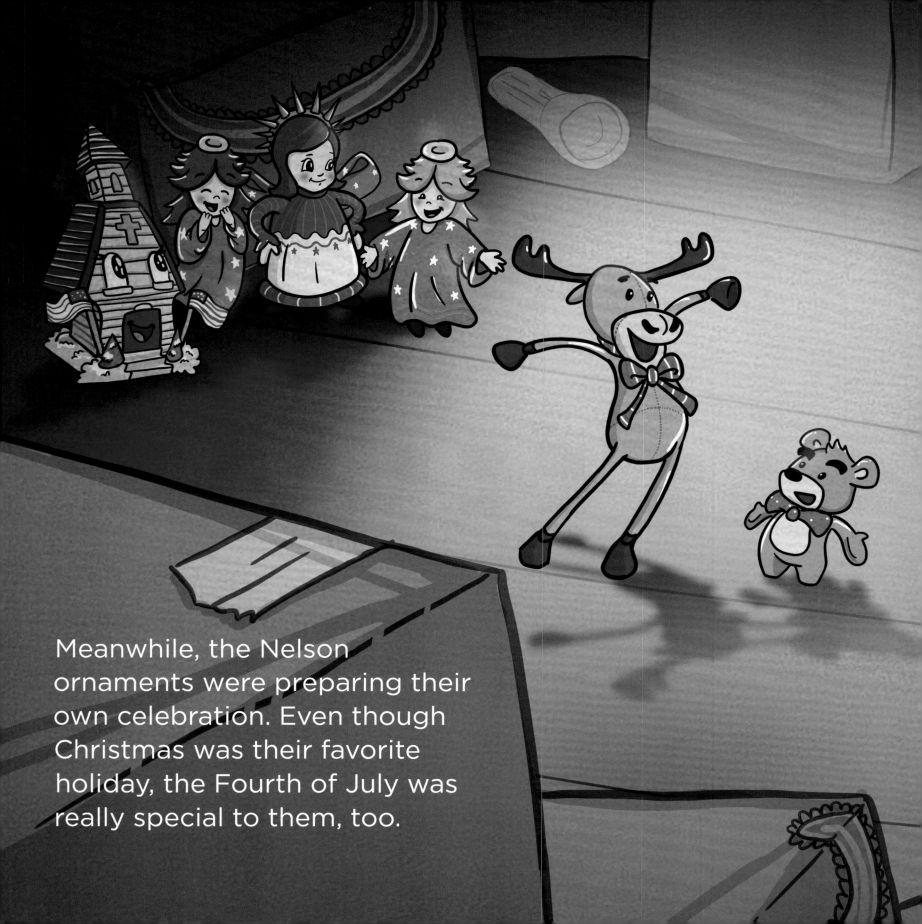

Meanwhile, the Nelson ornaments were preparing their own celebration. Even though Christmas was their favorite holiday, the Fourth of July was really special to them, too.

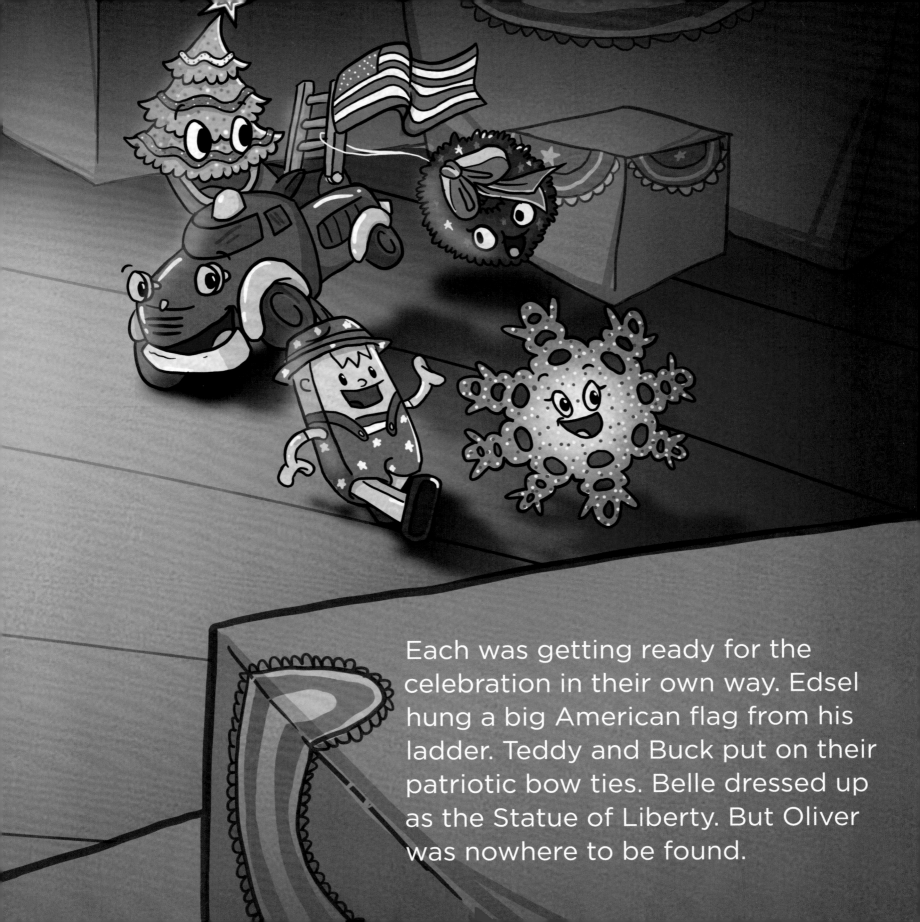

Each was getting ready for the celebration in their own way. Edsel hung a big American flag from his ladder. Teddy and Buck put on their patriotic bow ties. Belle dressed up as the Statue of Liberty. But Oliver was nowhere to be found.

"Oliver, where are you?" hollered Belle.

"Oliver, you're going to miss our practice," warned Abbey.

Then, from the back of the attic, out marched Oliver dressed from head to toe like Uncle Sam.

"You've outdone yourself this year, Oliver," said Marley and Joan, who had also gotten in the spirit with their own colorful outfits.

All the ornaments gathered together to make plans for the big day while admiring each other's Fourth of July costumes.

Back in the living room, Henry
and Holly were still playing on
their devices, and hadn't budged
an inch when Mom walked back in.
"Where are the flags?" she asked.

"Oh Mom, we're sorry, we just got really
busy playing..."

Mom interrupted Henry, took their devices,
and asked them once again to get the flags
from the attic.

On the way to the attic, Henry asked Holly... "Why
do they make such a big deal out of this anyhow?"
Holly agreed and wondered if they would ever get
their devices back.

Little did they know that they were soon going to find
out just what makes America so very special.

Meanwhile,
their friends
were lining up
for their special
Fourth of July parade.

Although Oliver normally served as the drum major
for the parade, this year he decided to give those
responsibilities to Norb.

"Norb," Oliver said, "you love America as much as the rest
of us, this year I think you should lead our parade."

An emotional Norb responded, "Thanks, Oliver. Even though
I'm not originally from here, I sure do love this country."

Marching in formation, the ornaments all began to play "Yankee Doodle Dandy." Two by two, they marched, playing their instruments and waving their flags.

Just then, Henry and Holly arrived, and couldn't believe their eyes. They knew the ornaments came to life in December through the magic of Christmas but had no idea they would see them in July.

"Oliver," shouted Henry, "What in the world are you doing?"

"Oh my," Holly added. "You're playing the song they taught us in school."

Henry and Holly sat down with their friends but were puzzled by their celebration of the Fourth of July.

"Oliver," Holly asked, "why are you making such a big deal out of this?"

"Yeah," added Henry. "It's just a day with fireworks and parades."

"Fireworks and parades are a *part* of the Fourth of July, but they're not *why* we celebrate this day," said Oliver.

"What do you mean?" asked Holly.

Oliver answered, "There are so many things to celebrate and honor on this day, like what great leaders we've had, or how many inspirational Americans there are for us to look up to and how as Americans we can accomplish anything we dream possible."

Henry said, "Sometimes they try to tell us some of these things in school, but it gets really boring."

"Boring?" Teddy asked. "Then you haven't really heard anything about what makes our nation so wonderful."

"Well," Holly said, "that's what Mom was trying to tell us this morning, Henry. Maybe our friends are right. Maybe we should listen a bit more."

Oliver began by saying, "One of the many great things we celebrate at this time of year is the amazing leaders we've had."

Dressed as George Washington, he and some of his friends reenacted the crossing of the Delaware and told the story of the American Revolution.

As Abraham Lincoln, he recited the Gettysburg Address. "Four score and seven years ago our fathers brought forth on this continent, a new nation, conceived in Liberty..."

Then he quoted even more inspirational words spoken by our nation's presidents.

"The only thing we have to fear is fear itself," Oliver recited the words of FDR.

"Ask not what your country can do for you—ask what you can do for your country," he continued, quoting from JFK's inauguration speech.

"Mr. Gorbachev, tear down this wall," Oliver concluded with the words of Ronald Reagan.

The other ornaments then joined Oliver, each telling stories of other historic Americans.

Frasier told the story of Martin Luther King Jr. and the bravery of Rosa Parks. Marley and Joan told them the story of Susan B. Anthony and her fight for women's equality. Edsel told them about the Greatest Generation and the sacrifices they made to save the world.

Then they told stories of the beauty of America.

Teddy and Norb began by showing them pictures of the Grand Canyon and the rolling farmland of Wisconsin.

Abbey showed them pictures of the beautiful coastline in California and some of the greatest cities in the world, like Chicago and New York.

And Oliver finished by telling them all about the beauty of all of our national parks.

Edsel then drove to the front, saying, "I want to tell you about all of America's great innovations and inventions. These are things we also celebrate."

He then continued. "More than fifty years ago, Americans were the very first to land on the moon," began Edsel. "Then there's my favorite inventor, Henry Ford."

He finished with stories from the cotton gin to the internet.

"You see," said Edsel, "Americans have accomplished and invented some of the greatest things in the history of the world."

Then Abbey came forward to talk about what makes America so important to her.

"In America," Abbey began, "we are free to worship any way we choose, we can assemble anywhere we want, we can believe anything we choose, and we have the freedom to express our own opinions.

"No other country has given so many rights to their people than America," Abbey concluded.

Henry and Holly now understood why the Fourth of July and America were so important. They asked to hear more stories, but just then they heard a loud gust of wind, sounding as if it was going to blow down the entire house.

Frasier looked out the attic window and screamed, "Oh no!"

The family flag had come loose and blown into the air. It was headed for the ground.

Edsel was quick on his feet and asked Henry and Holly to remove his ladder and push it out the window. As they did, all of the ornaments slid down it to the catch the flag.

"Just in time," a relieved Oliver exclaimed. Looking up at Henry and Holly as they raised the flag, Oliver hollered, "Never let the flag hit the ground!"

Holly and Henry were amazed at just how much America and the flag meant to their friends. Now they were beginning to understand why.

Once back in the attic the children asked to hear more stories.

Oliver finished by saying, "Henry and Holly, in America you can accomplish anything you dream possible. Henry, you can be a fireman or a surgeon. Holly, you could be the first person to land on Mars or a police officer. It's all up to you."

Henry's and Holly's imaginations went wild.

"First person on Mars... I like that," Holly thought.

"A firefighter—how great would that be," Henry dreamed.

Henry and Holly thanked their friends, but before saying good-bye, joined them in the parade. This time, instead of singing "Yankee Doodle Dandy," they changed the words to "Oliver Doodle Dandy."

Henry and Holly put on patriotic shirts, then returned downstairs with their flags in hand and their hearts and minds filled with love, respect, and admiration for America.

Mom thanked Henry and Holly for bringing the flags and gave their devices back to them. But Henry and Holly didn't want them.

"Can we help Daddy put up the flags, Mom?" asked Holly.

Mom was surprised but delighted. "Of course you can."

As Henry and Holly walked outside, Mom overheard Henry say, "Remember, you can't let the flag hit the ground."

Once outside, they started putting up flag after flag throughout their yard. As they did, they looked up at Oliver, who waved back and winked at both of them.

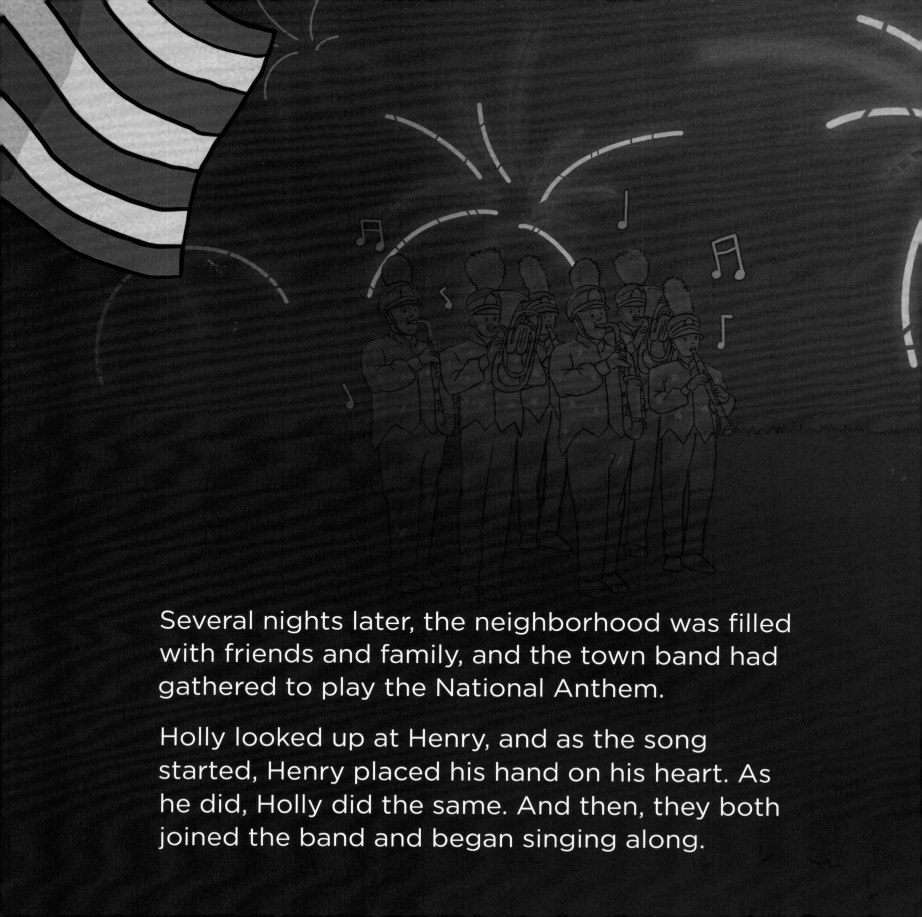

Several nights later, the neighborhood was filled with friends and family, and the town band had gathered to play the National Anthem.

Holly looked up at Henry, and as the song started, Henry placed his hand on his heart. As he did, Holly did the same. And then, they both joined the band and began singing along.

As the fireworks began, Henry and Holly looked up at the attic. In the window was each of their friends, watching the same display. Holly and Henry now realized what made this day so special and were eager to learn even more about their great country, the United States of America.

Several weeks later...

Several weeks later, Mom and Dad walked up behind Henry and Holly, who were both on their devices. "Look Mom," said Dad, "they're playing those games again." Much to their surprise, they saw that Holly was reading all about Mars, while Henry was reading a story about Henry Ford.

"Hmm," said Mom. "I wonder what's gotten into them?"

Sing Along with Oliver Doodle Dandy

MY COUNTRY 'TIS OF THEE

My country, 'tis of thee,
Sweet land of liberty,
Of thee I sing;
Land where my fathers died,
Land of the Pilgrims' pride,
From every mountain-side
Let Freedom ring.

THIS IS MY COUNTRY

This is my country!
Land of my birth!
This is my country!
Grandest on earth!
I pledge thee my allegiance,
America, the bold,
For this is my country
to have and to hold.

YANKEE DOODLE DANDY

Yankee Doodle went to town
A-riding on a pony,
Stuck a feather in his cap
And called it macaroni.

Chorus:
Yankee Doodle keep it up,
Yankee Doodle dandy,
Mind the music and the step,
And with the girls be handy.

Fath'r and I went down to camp,
Along with Captain Gooding,
And there we saw the men and boys
As thick as hasty pudding.

THIS LAND IS YOUR LAND

This land is your land, this land is my land
From California to the New York Island
From the Redwood Forest to the Gulf
Stream waters
This land was made for you and me.

As I was walking that ribbon of highway
I saw above me that endless skyway
I saw below me that golden valley
This land was made for you and me.

STAR SPANGLED BANNER

Oh, say can you see by the dawn's early light
What so proudly we hailed at the twilight's last gleaming?
Whose broad stripes and bright stars thru the perilous fight,
O'er the ramparts we watched were so gallantly streaming?
And the rocket's red glare, the bombs bursting in air,
Gave proof through the night that our flag was still there.
Oh, say does that star-spangled banner yet wave
O'er the land of the free and the home of the brave?

YOU'RE A GRAND OLD FLAG

You're a grand old flag,
You're a high flying flag
And forever in peace may you wave.
You're the emblem of
The land I love.
The home of the free and the brave.
Ev'ry heart beats true
'neath the Red, White and Blue,
Where there's never a boast or brag.
Should auld acquaintance be forgot,
Keep your eye on the grand old flag

AMERICA THE BEAUTIFUL

O beautiful for spacious skies,
For amber waves of grain,
For purple mountain
majesties
Above the fruited plain!
America! America!
God shed his grace on thee
And crown thy good with
brotherhood
From sea to shining sea!

O beautiful for pilgrim feet
Whose stern impassioned
stress
A thoroughfare of freedom
beat
Across the wilderness!
America! America!
God mend thine every flaw,
Confirm thy soul in self-
control,
Thy liberty in law!

GOD BLESS AMERICA

God Bless America,
Land that I love
Stand beside her,
And guide her,
Through the night
With the light from above,
From the mountains,
To the prairies,
To the ocean,
White with foam,
God bless America,
My home sweet home.
God bless America,
My home sweet home.

What I Love About America

What I Love About America

DISCOVER THE MAGIC OF

Oliver The Ornament™

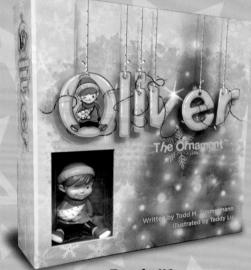

Book #2
Hard-Bound Book
AVAILABLE NOW

Book #1
Gift Set
AVAILABLE NOW

Book #3
Hard-Bound Book
AVAILABLE CHRISTMAS 2020

Oliver the Ornament is a seven-book series about one family's collection of ornaments.

Each book shares the magical tale of how the ornaments entered the family's collection, each teaches children the message of kindness, and each ends with a cliff-hanger, exciting everyone for what's to come.

Begin a new family tradition with Oliver the Ornament this Christmas. Available at fine retailers everywhere and at www.olivertheornament.com

Book #4 – Oliver the Ornament Meets Frasier and Merry.
Available Christmas 2021

Book #5 – Oliver the Ornament Meets Norb and Teddy.
Available Christmas 2022

Book #6 – Oliver the Ornament Meets Buck, Edsel, and Crystal.
Available Christmas 2023

Book #7 – Oliver the Ornament Meets...
Available Christmas 2024

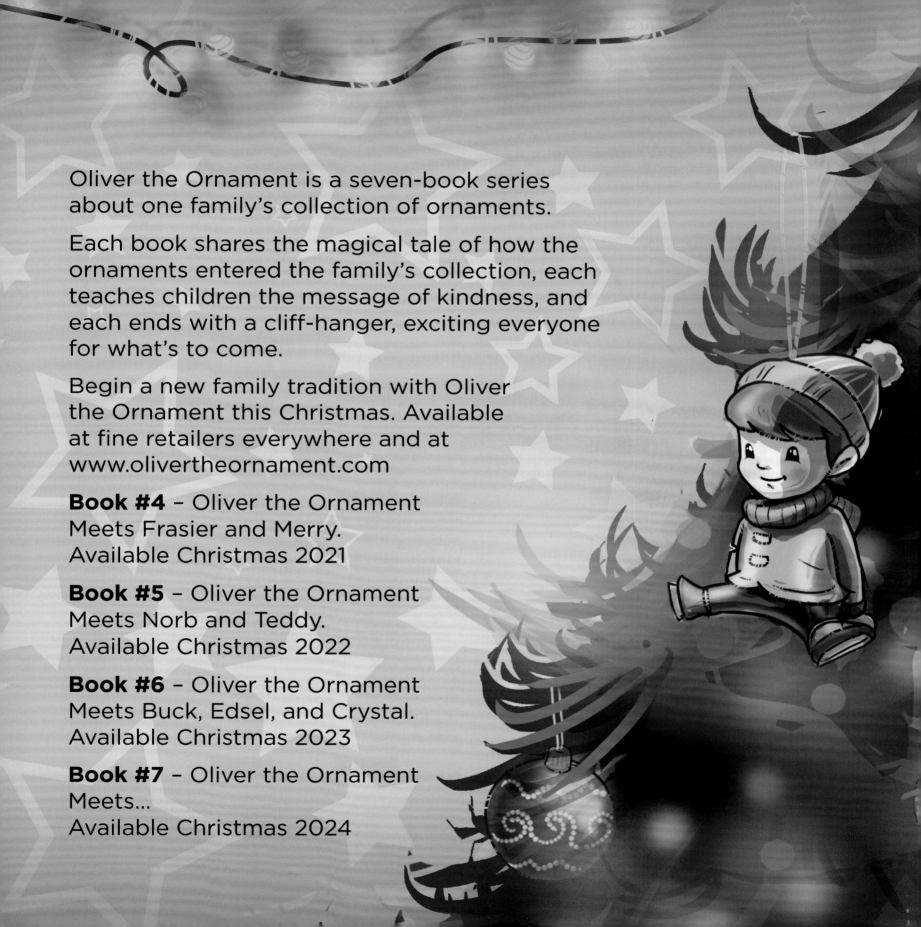

With grateful appreciation to Mindy Bertka, Todd Kibbey, Gary Gronlund, Tom and Denise Kazar, Pete and Karen Krochmolny, Diana Laskaris, Kris and Mike McLean, Tom O'Reilly, Rose and Ron Ostermann, Cheryl Reed, Loreen Strasser, Aurora and Chris Swehla, Tom Trucco, Caryn Weiss, Dave and Heidi Zimmermann.

With the biggest thanks and appreciation reserved for John Hoerst.

In loving memory of our friends and family no longer with us, including: Myron Heffernan, Mary Jane Hemssing, John LaGrassa, Fred Mendell, John Piccolo, Phil Reynolds, Ross Rottmann, Matt Snyder, Bill Sutmar, Doris Zimmermann and Oliver's biggest cheerleader, Marlene Zimmermann.

Oliver & Friends, Inc.
P.O. Box 13304
Chicago, IL   60613

www.olivertheornament.com

ISBN 978-0-9863416-6-3

Printed in China.